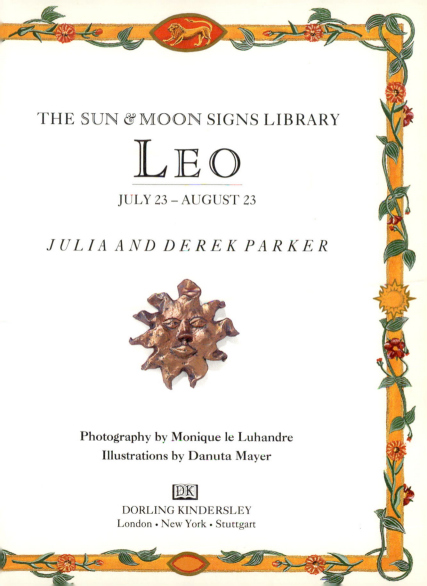

THE SUN & MOON SIGNS LIBRARY

# LEO

JULY 23 – AUGUST 23

*JULIA AND DEREK PARKER*

Photography by Monique le Luhandre
Illustrations by Danuta Mayer

DK

DORLING KINDERSLEY
London · New York · Stuttgart

*Dedicated to Joan and Alan Smith*

A DORLING KINDERSLEY BOOK

Editor **Tom Fraser**
Art Editor **Ursula Dawson**
Managing Editor **Krystyna Mayer**
Managing Art Editor **Derek Coombes**
Production **Antony Heller**
U.S. Editor **Laaren Brown**

Computer page make-up Patrizio Semproni.
Photography p 11 © Michael Holford/British Museum; p 16 Tim Ridley.
Stylist pp 28-29 Lucy Elworthy. Illustration pp 60-61 Kuo Kang Chen.
Jacket illustration Peter Lawman. With thanks to Carolyn
Lancaster and John Filbey.

First American Edition, 1992
10 9 8 7 6 5 4 3 2 1

Published in the United States by
Dorling Kindersley, Inc., 232 Madison Avenue
New York, N.Y. 10016

Library of Congress Catalog Card Number 92-52788
ISBN 1-56458-088-1

Reproduced by GRB Editrice, Verona, Italy
Printed and bound in Hong Kong by Imago

# CONTENTS

# *INTRODUCING*
# LEO

LEO, THE SIGN OF THE LION AND KING OF BEASTS, IS THE
FIFTH SIGN OF THE ZODIAC. LEOS USUALLY MANAGE
TO ACQUIRE THEIR OWN INDIVIDUAL KINGDOMS OVER WHICH
THEY CAN RULE SUPREME.

The Zodiac lion or lioness rules skillfully, tactfully organizing others and always expressing creativity in one form or another.

This sign is ruled by the Sun. In fact, it is almost as if the generous, bright Leo personality radiates from some inner sun. When such a forceful personality fails to shine through, one can tell that something is seriously wrong. Leos who suppress their inner glow will be unhappy and unable to fully express their potential.

### Traditional groupings
As you read through this book you will come across references to the elements and the qualities, and to positive and negative, or masculine and feminine signs.

The first of these groupings, that of the elements, comprises fire, earth, air, and water signs. The second, that of the qualities, divides the Zodiac into cardinal, fixed, and mutable signs. The final grouping is made up of positive and negative, or masculine and feminine signs. Each Zodiac sign is associated with a combination of components from these groupings, all of which contribute different characteristics to it.

### Leo characteristics
Leo is of the fixed quality, which means that while Leos are generally stable people, they can also be very stubborn. They work hard to curb any tendency toward being bossy or pompous, and limit their urge to overdramatize every problem.

Because Leo is a masculine, positive sign, it inclines its subjects to be extroverted. Another characteristic that makes Leos easy to identify is their enthusiasm. This is, in fact, indicative of the sign's element: fire.

Most Leos will prefer, and perhaps enjoy wearing, the opulent colors of the Sun, their ruling "planet."

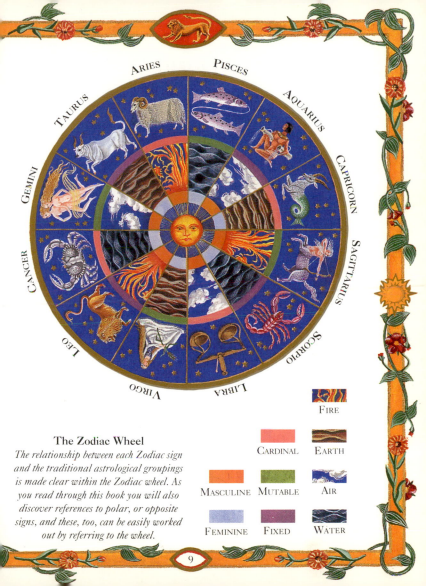

### The Zodiac Wheel

*The relationship between each Zodiac sign and the traditional astrological groupings is made clear within the Zodiac wheel. As you read through this book you will also discover references to polar, or opposite signs, and these, too, can be easily worked out by referring to the wheel.*

FIRE

CARDINAL    EARTH

MASCULINE    MUTABLE    AIR

FEMININE    FIXED    WATER

# MYTHS & LEGENDS

THE ZODIAC, WHICH IS BELIEVED TO HAVE ORIGINATED IN
BABYLON AS LONG AS 2,500 YEARS AGO, IS A
CIRCLE OF CONSTELLATIONS THROUGH WHICH THE SUN
MOVES DURING THE COURSE OF A YEAR.

When the major stars of the constellation Leo are joined together, they do actually resemble a crouching beast. The ancient Babylonians called the constellation Great Dog. At least 5,000 years ago, the Egyptians gave it the name that is familiar to us today.

## The Labors of Hercules

Like the Crab of Cancer, the Lion is associated with one of the 12 labors that the hero Hercules was made to perform by King Eurystheus, the ruler of Greece, as an atonement for slaughtering his own wife and children. After consulting the Oracle at Delphi, Hercules learned that only by showing obedience to King Eurystheus could he ever be forgiven for his dastardly crime.

Hercules's first labor involved killing and flaying an enormous lion, whose pelt was so tough that it could turn aside all weapons.

## The Nemean lion

The lion, which lived at Nemea, in the Peloponnese, was born of Echidna the snake-woman and Typhon, a monster with a hundred eyes. The goddess Hera had sent it to wreak havoc upon the neighborhood of Nemea, the plain of which was sacred to Zeus, king of the gods.

Meeting the lion on the slopes of Mount Tretus, Hercules first shot at it with arrows (it merely yawned as they rebounded from its skin), then attacked it with his sword, and finally struck it with his club. At this point, irritated by a headache, it bit off one of Hercules's fingers.

Hercules eventually resorted to the novel idea of choking the lion to death while it was resting in its cave. On trying to skin it, however, he found that its hide resisted all knives, so that he eventually had to use its own claws – the only instruments sharp enough. Hercules subsequently

**Hercules and the Nemean Lion**
*This Greek vase, which dates from 510 B.C., shows
Hercules struggling to overcome the seemingly
invincible Nemean lion.*

wore the lion's impenetrable skin as armor, with the head as a helmet. The lion itself was set in effigy among the stars by Zeus.

### Leo characteristics

It is, of course, virtually impossible to determine how various human qualities became associated with a particular sign of the Zodiac. It can, however, be said that those born with the Sun in Leo are extremely likely to possess the unmistakably proud demeanor of lions, and that they seem to be just as invulnerable to attack. Indeed, bravery, strong leadership, and forcefulness of personality are all definite Leo characteristics. However, when Leos find themselves troubled, they will retire to some private place in order to recover from their wounds in solitude.

# *LEO*
# SYMBOLISM

CERTAIN HERBS, SPICES, FLOWERS, TREES, GEMS, METALS,
AND ANIMALS HAVE LONG BEEN ASSOCIATED WITH
PARTICULAR ZODIAC SIGNS. SOME ASSOCIATIONS ARE SIMPLY
AMUSING, WHILE OTHERS CAN BE USEFUL.

**Flowers**

*The sunflower, marigold, and
celandine, all of which reflect the
vibrant colors of this sign, are
ruled by Leo.*

MARIGOLDS

SUNFLOWERS

## Herbs

*All herbs are believed to be ruled by Leo. This is particularly true of angelica, which "comforts the heart"; eyebright, which is good for eye ailments; and pimpernel, which alleviates toothache.*

BAY

ANGELICA

## Trees

*The bay, palm, and walnut are traditionally Leo trees. The same is true for the orange, lemon, and all other citrus trees.*

ARECA PALM

## Spices

*No spices are specifically connected with Leo. As a fire sign, however, Leo surely rules pepper and mustard.*

MUSTARD

PEPPER

BRASS LION'S-HEAD DOOR KNOCKER

### Animals
*The lion is, naturally, the Leo
animal, but all other big cats are also
ruled by this sign.*

DIAMANTÉ TIGER BROOCH

### Metal
*Gold is the Leo metal, not only
because of its association with the
Sun, but also because of Leo's
unquestionable taste for riches.*

WOODEN TIGER
FOLK CARVING

GOLD

LEOPARD CIGARETTE LIGHTER

RUBY EARRINGS

RUBY BROOCH

TOY TIN LION

RUBY NECKLACE

**Gem**
*The dark red, glowing ruby, the
color of the Sun at dusk, is ruled
by this sign.*

# LEO
# PROFILE

THE LION'S MANE OF HAIR, THE UPRIGHT STANCE, AND A RATHER
CONVENTIONAL, BUT VERY DASHING IMAGE, CHARACTERIZE
THIS DRAMATIC ZODIAC SIGN. LEOS MAY SOMETIMES CONVEY AN
IMAGE OF HAUGHTINESS TO OTHERS.

Sun sign Leos stand with their feet placed slightly apart and their legs held straight. They tend to make strong, meaningful gestures that are carried through in a distinctive and often dramatic way.

### The body
Generally speaking, the Leo spine and back are erect, which gives people of this sign the appearance of height even if they are not tall. Leos are typically broad shouldered, and most have admirably slim waists. This can be a decided asset when fashion decrees an emphasis on that area. Leos usually move well, and should aim to keep their elegant, cat-like agility well into old age. Your feet and hands are unlikely to be large,

**The Leo face**
*You are likely to have a noble face, with bright, clear eyes.*

and you will probably be small boned in comparison to members of most other Zodiac sign groups.

### The face
You will hold your head high. If you leave your hair to grow long it will probably become as luxuriant and flowing as a lion's mane, although it may sometimes be equally untamable. Most Leos have clear complexions, and are likely to tan well. There is a striking nobility about the Leo forehead and face that you may well possess. Your eyes are likely to be very bright and clear, with perhaps slightly drooping eyelids, and your nose may be large and prominent. Some Leos develop a habit of occasionally looking down

### The Leo stance

*In keeping with their outgoing manner, Leos stand well, and are prone to making bold, meaningful gestures.*

their noses at other people. You will not find it hard to break into a wide, sunny smile.

### Style

Of all the Sun signs, Leo probably has the best sense of style. Since most Leos enjoy making a dramatic impact, there is often something eye-catching or spectacular about the things that they decide to wear.

Designer jeans and designer labels are very popular among Leos. However, people of this sign should make sure that they control their showiness, since too much glitter can ruin their image. Similarly, although Leos are generally inclined to buy high-quality, slightly conservative clothes, many of them will rashly spend enormous sums of money on dazzling but terribly impractical outfits that they can only wear once. Most Leos learn with experience.

People of your Sun sign usually look marvelous in the colors of the Sun, from palest lemon and pink to darkest orange, with younger people liking the brightest colors.

### In general

Because the Leo body reflects the Leo psychology, it is not difficult to tell how happy a Leo is. It is obvious that a round-shouldered, stooping Leo, with eyes dimmed, is burdened with problems. On the other hand, if Leos are upright and smiling, their psychological Sun, which is so much a part of every Leo, is quite clearly shining, and all is well.

# *LEO*
# PERSONALITY

GENEROSITY AND ENTHUSIASM ARE BOTH DOMINANT LEO
TRAITS. WHILE LEOS ENJOY TAKING CENTER STAGE,
THEY WILL ALSO ENCOURAGE THEIR LOVED ONES AND
FRIENDS TO GET THE MOST OUT OF LIFE.

Being positive and enthusiastic in outlook, Leos have a great zest for life, and if only because they put so much into it in the first place, they will get a great deal out of it. Every day has to be lived to the fullest. Inner satisfaction comes when you settle down to relax at the end of the day and realize that not only has each of your tasks been well and truly completed, but also that there is something to show for all your efforts.

## At work

As a Sun sign Leo, your organizing ability is almost certain to be excellent. You can, however, sometimes express your love for organization in an extremely bossy way. This tendency to become too dominant over people must be controlled if it is not to be a source of embarrassment to your family and friends. Should you find yourself in charge of a situation (as Leos so often

are), you should make sure that you hand out instructions with as much charm and warmth as you can. Bear in mind that other people thrive on receiving encouragement and praise, just as you do.

## Your attitudes

Leos are known to hate pettiness of any kind. You will be very good at comprehending the overall plan and concept of a project, but will then willingly leave the smaller, fussy details to other people. Small-minded behavior and nit-picking arguments will no doubt infuriate you. When you encounter these, what might very accurately be called your "lion's roar" will be heard, and you will put the culprits in their place.

Leos usually have a well-developed sense of drama, which definitely needs to be tempered with a little restraint. At its best, however, it will provide you with a great

**The Sun rules Leo**

*Apollo, the Greek Sun god, represents the Sun that rules over Leo. The Sun inclines its subjects to be generous, affectionate, and creative.*

awareness of occasion. You will have no trouble making something special out of every get-together that you are party to, and you will really love to entertain extravagantly.

**The overall picture**

Firmness, determination, and decisiveness are marvelous qualities. Dogmatism and stubbornness are, however, just the opposite. You must tread very carefully in this area. Although it can be very difficult for you to develop an ability to be flexible, it will help if you consciously remember that the best rulers are those who are understanding, reasonable, and fair – especially when they are pronouncing judgment on other people.

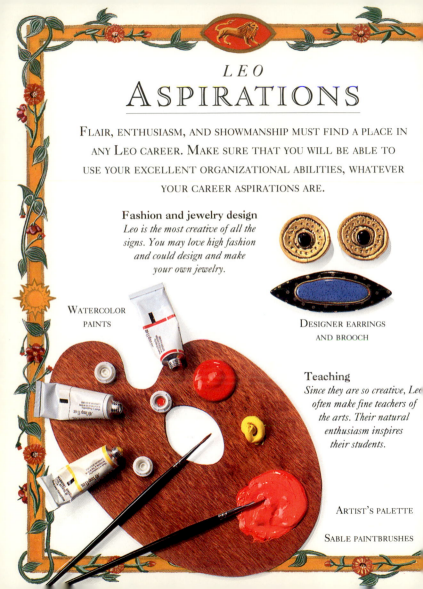

## LEO
# ASPIRATIONS

FLAIR, ENTHUSIASM, AND SHOWMANSHIP MUST FIND A PLACE IN ANY LEO CAREER. MAKE SURE THAT YOU WILL BE ABLE TO USE YOUR EXCELLENT ORGANIZATIONAL ABILITIES, WHATEVER YOUR CAREER ASPIRATIONS ARE.

### Fashion and jewelry design
*Leo is the most creative of all the signs. You may love high fashion and could design and make your own jewelry.*

WATERCOLOR
PAINTS

DESIGNER EARRINGS
AND BROOCH

### Teaching
*Since they are so creative, Leo often make fine teachers of the arts. Their natural enthusiasm inspires their students.*

ARTIST'S PALETTE

SABLE PAINTBRUSHES

**V**ENETIAN
**FESTIVAL**
**MASK**

## The theater

*A career in the theater, which would
combine a number of the qualities
traditionally associated with
Leo, may strongly
appeal to you.*

1912 FOOTBALL MEDAL
**R**EFEREE'S WHISTLE

## Professional sports

*Leos find sports and
exercise important, and like to take a pride in
their bodies. You could therefore find the idea
of a career in professional sport attractive.*

**L**EAD SOLDIERS

## The armed forces

*Leos have great powers of leadership. You
may do well in the armed services and
could rise to a position of authority.*

## Illustration

*Leos often turn their artistic
talents to illustrative
drawing or painting.*

**C**HARCOAL

# HEALTH

MORE THAN ANY OTHER ZODIAC TYPE, LEO NEEDS TO BE SOUND IN
BOTH MIND AND BODY; THEY ARE UNIQUELY CONNECTED
IN THIS SIGN. FOR EXAMPLE, AN INJURED BACK COULD LEAD TO
DEPRESSION, OR A PRESSING PROBLEM, A HEADACHE.

The lions of the Zodiac will rapidly fall into black moods if some injury threatens to cramp their action-packed lives. You will become angry with yourself if such an injury forces you to stay away from your health club, and your irritation with an injury may far outweigh your pain or discomfort. This is because you really do not like wasting time or neglecting something you love doing. Rather fortunately for you, and perhaps for those who know you, such situations do not arise all that often.

### Your diet
Mineral salts are considered to be a necessary part of the human diet. Because of modern eating habits, however, our supply of them is often unbalanced. As a Sun sign Leo you may benefit from supplementing your diet with the cell salt magnesium phosphate (mag. phos.). This is good for the heart, and helps to aid relaxation. You should also make sure that you control the amount of cholesterol you consume.

### Taking care
The Leo body area is the spine and back. Chairs that offer good support are an excellent idea. So are exercises geared to strengthening the back; these will help you to avoid backache – often just a sign of stress. The Leo organ, the heart, also needs to be exercised if it is to be kept in good shape like the rest of the body.

Leos are usually strong and healthy, with mind and body at one with each other. You must be careful that you do not use up your energy – you might be forced to take a rest. Maintaining a balance is therefore of above average importance for you. Of course, you should be careful not to lose sight of the fact that when you do set aside some time to relax, you will enjoy it with all of your Leo panache.

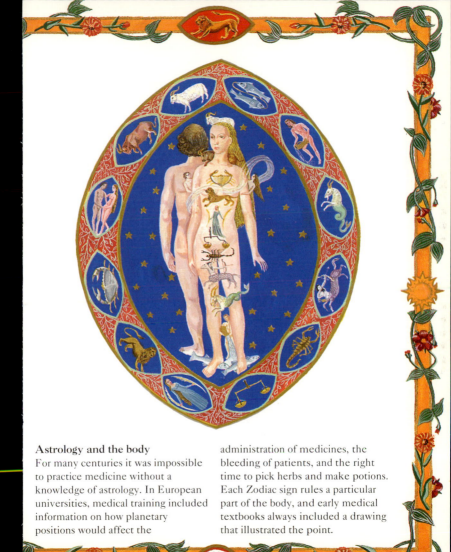

### Astrology and the body

For many centuries it was impossible to practice medicine without a knowledge of astrology. In European universities, medical training included information on how planetary positions would affect the administration of medicines, the bleeding of patients, and the right time to pick herbs and make potions. Each Zodiac sign rules a particular part of the body, and early medical textbooks always included a drawing that illustrated the point.

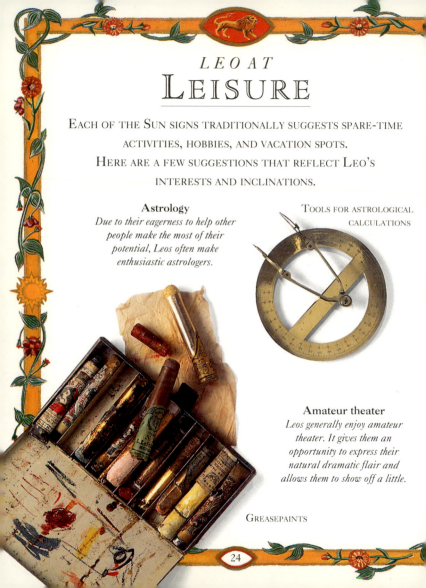

### LEO AT
# LEISURE

Each of the Sun signs traditionally suggests spare-time
activities, hobbies, and vacation spots.
Here are a few suggestions that reflect Leo's
interests and inclinations.

### Astrology

*Due to their eagerness to help other
people make the most of their
potential, Leos often make
enthusiastic astrologers.*

Tools for astrological
calculations

### Amateur theater

*Leos generally enjoy amateur
theater. It gives them an
opportunity to express their
natural dramatic flair and
allows them to show off a little.*

Greasepaints

PLASTER IMAGE
OF THE SUN

POSTAGE STAMPS

## Travel

*Comfort, even luxury, should be the
hallmark of your holiday. You would
rather spend a day in a five-star hotel
than a month in a tent. Italy, Iraq,
the South of France, and the Alps
all appeal to Leo.*

## The Sun

*Leos love enjoying the Sun. Its
light and warmth give them a sense
of well-being, making them feel
positive and optimistic.*

NAPKIN
AND CUTLERY

## Eating out

*You no doubt have a great
sense of style and occasion,
and therefore only the best will
be good enough for you when
you choose to eat out.*

# LEO IN
# LOVE

WHEN LEO FALLS IN LOVE, THE WORLD TAKES ON A GOLDEN
GLOW – BUT WHEN LEO IS REJECTED OR UNLUCKY IN
LOVE, THE STORM CLOUDS GATHER. ANY WOUNDS ARE LICKED
IN THE PRIVACY OF THE LAIR.

Sun sign Leos tend to put their partners on pedestals. You may be the king or queen of the Zodiac, but you will also enjoy playing consort to your partners. This means that when things go wrong, you may suffer more than most Zodiac types. Disillusion and heartbreak are common, and are sometimes followed by a loss of self-confidence that only time can heal. Unfortunately, some Leos are psychologically less developed than others and will tend to dominate a weak partner. At times this may work, if that partner is the type who needs a great deal of support, but both parties must aim to achieve a balanced relationship based upon sharing.

The generosity attributed to Leo will certainly be expressed when you are in love. The wrong partner may feel that you are showing off or trying to impress. This is not the case: with you "celebration" is the key word, and to blazes with the cost.

### As a lover
The fire element of Leo burns strongly and brightly when you realize that you are in love. You will want your partner to share the sheer joy and exuberance of your

positive expression of emotion, through psychological rapport and friendship as well as through rewarding and fulfilling sex. It is equally important for all Leos to have partners who are able to share an enthusiasm for their interests.

## Types of Leo lover

Many Leos are flirtatious, enjoying a powerful bond of friendship as well as love and romance. They need partners who are their intellectual equals. Other Sun sign Leos are very sentimental. They may tend to create a claustrophobic atmosphere within a relationship and, should a partner decide to break away, will find it difficult to accept the fact that the romance has ended. Many Leos are totally leonine in their

expression of love: When in love, life for them becomes one huge, romantic musical, opera, or film. Some other Leos display, very surprisingly, a certain modesty in this sphere of their lives. Finally, there are those Leos who are never really psychologically whole until they are sharing their life with a partner. Premature commitment can be a real danger for these types.

## LEO AT
# HOME

A LEO'S WARM AND WELL-LIT HOME WILL REFLECT THE HIGHEST
STANDARDS OF COMFORT. ELEGANCE, STYLE, AND BEAUTY
ARE THE KEYNOTES AND, EVEN ON SLENDER MEANS, THEY WILL
USUALLY BE ACHIEVED.

Wherever Sun sign Leos end up living, they always strive to make their homes very special places. You will probably spend a great deal of money on beautiful things, and on improving your home, for precisely this reason. If you have a garden, you have probably filled it with many different types of colorful flowers, and if the climate permits, attractive exotic fruits and vegetables. Your entire home is likely to have a warm and glowing atmosphere.

**Classical sculpture**
*Leos often own a copy of
an ancient sculpture.*

### Furniture

When it comes to choosing furniture for your home, your decisions are probably based around elegance and comfort. Leos like to relax in beautiful surroundings that are stylish, luxurious, and easy on the eye. You take great pride in your home, and will, as has already been said, spend a lot of money on it, making sure that the furniture and decor you choose is unlikely to become boring after a year or two. In this way you will avoid the disruption of the constant necessity for change. Quality is likely to be very important to you, and Leos sometimes have a marked tendency toward showiness that should be controlled. You may, for instance, overdo a room by placing too much elaborate and obviously expensive furniture together, and perhaps in inappropriate places.

### Exotic wallpaper
*Leo furnishings are often striking, like this*
*wallpaper in the style of William Morris.*

### Soft furnishings
Texture and warm, glowing color are
both important: many Leos favor rich
silks and brocades, or velvet which
will deepen and enhance the colors
that they choose. Although you may
be very much attracted to fur rugs,
Leos are among the leaders in the
conservation of wildlife, and are
especially sympathetic toward the big
cats. No self-respecting Leo would
decide to own a real lion- or tiger-skin
rug; it will have to be a very high-
quality imitation.

### Decorative objects
Only the best is good enough for
Leos, whatever decorative objects
they may choose. Therefore one finds
ornaments in the Leo home that are
as near to perfection as can be
afforded, and some that may have
strained the individual's purse-strings.
　Your glass will be the finest crystal,
and the paintings, will be beautifully
framed. Leos like classical things, so a
reproduction of a Greek sculpture or a
miniature copy of some noble Roman
emperor sitting in triumph on his
horse may also make an appearance.

### Colorful armchair and cushion
*The golden colors of this chair and*
*cushion reflect the colors of the sun, which*
*are so dear to Leos.*

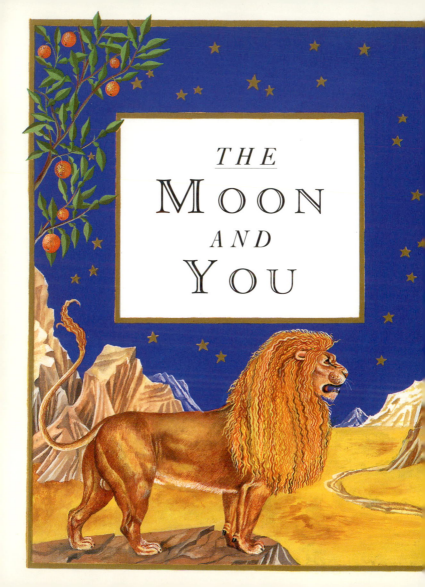

# THE
# MOON
## AND
# YOU

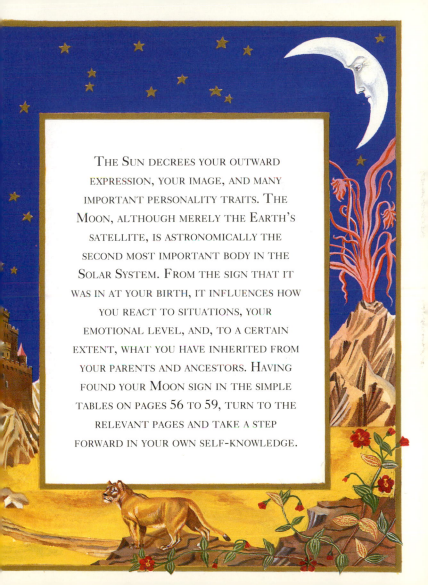

THE SUN DECREES YOUR OUTWARD
EXPRESSION, YOUR IMAGE, AND MANY
IMPORTANT PERSONALITY TRAITS. THE
MOON, ALTHOUGH MERELY THE EARTH'S
SATELLITE, IS ASTRONOMICALLY THE
SECOND MOST IMPORTANT BODY IN THE
SOLAR SYSTEM. FROM THE SIGN THAT IT
WAS IN AT YOUR BIRTH, IT INFLUENCES HOW
YOU REACT TO SITUATIONS, YOUR
EMOTIONAL LEVEL, AND, TO A CERTAIN
EXTENT, WHAT YOU HAVE INHERITED FROM
YOUR PARENTS AND ANCESTORS. HAVING
FOUND YOUR MOON SIGN IN THE SIMPLE
TABLES ON PAGES 56 TO 59, TURN TO THE
RELEVANT PAGES AND TAKE A STEP
FORWARD IN YOUR OWN SELF-KNOWLEDGE.

# THE MOON IN
# ARIES

A COMBINATION OF TWO FIRE SIGNS GIVES YOU A HIGH LEVEL OF
PHYSICAL AND EMOTIONAL ENERGY, BUT YOU MUST LEARN
TO CURB HASTINESS AND SELFISH REACTIONS TO PARTNERS. YOU
ARE MORE CASUAL THAN MOST LEOS.

Basically, you are a very energetic person with a powerful motivation to win, and your Leo organizational ability will enable you to take over any critical situation at the drop of a hat.

### Self-expression

You will, unfortunately, express Leo bossiness from time to time. But the lively, positive influence of your Arien Moon makes it unlikely that you will come to annoy other people too much. Your Arien Moon will also mitigate any Leo pomposity.

You should avoid being too hasty, since this could lead you into premature and ill-considered action. Learn from your past mistakes and pace yourself. You may not be too good at coping with detail; perhaps you need the help of others once you have mapped out an overall plan. You have formidable resources of energy, and could easily have a hot temper.

However, neither Aries nor Leo harbors resentment, and Leo magnanimity usually emerges soon after any explosion of anger.

### Romance

Your Arien Moon makes you a very passionate and lively lover, and your natural *joie de vivre* is both infectious and attractive. The worst Arien fault can be selfishness, and this trait is not at all endearing.

You are among the most highly sexed of Leos and will probably fall in love at first sight. You will expect an equally positive and immediate response from prospective partners. Remember that not everyone is as sure of their feelings as you, and try to develop patience.

### Your well-being

The Arien body area is the head, and you may suffer from an above-average number of headaches. Often these

## The Moon in Aries

will be caused by other people. Arien headaches may also sometimes be caused by slight kidney disorders.

You are probably somewhat accident-prone, because of hastiness and your quick reactions. Take care in dangerous circumstances.

### Planning ahead

Your Arien Moon can make you somewhat impulsive financially, and you may tend to put too many eggs in one basket if you are convinced that an investment will be lucrative. A little caution is advisable, since over-enthusiasm could be your downfall.

### Parenthood

You will be among the most enthusiastic and encouraging of parents, making time to enjoy your children and seeing to it that their out-of-school life is full of activity. Learn to enthuse about their projects, and you will have fun. You should have no generation gap problems.

# THE MOON IN
# TAURUS

LEO LIKES THE BEST AND MOST EXPENSIVE OF EVERYTHING. YOUR
TAUREAN MOON IS IN SYMPATHY. SINCE YOU NEED MONEY
FOR ALL THOSE LUXURIES, TRY TO DEVELOP YOUR BUSINESS SENSE.
MAKE AN EFFORT NOT TO BE FLASHY.

You are lucky, since in astrology the Moon is said to be "well placed" in Taurus. This means that it will exert a strong influence upon you. Your Moon sign will make you very reliable and dependable.

## Self-expression

You need an above-average sense of emotional and financial security; if you have both, you will flourish.

Your Leo liking for luxury and quality will certainly be enhanced by your Taurean Moon since, after Leo, Taurus is the sign of the Zodiac most inclined toward such pleasurable things. Your Taurean Moon makes you practical and down-to-earth, and you will work hard and persistently to achieve your objectives.

## Romance

Your Leo passion is enhanced by Taurean sensuality, and you are usually faithful. But you must remain aware that the worst Taurean fault, possessiveness, can very easily overcome you. Try to counter this negative trait with Leo magnanimity.

## Your well-being

The Taurean body area is the throat. If your particular love is singing, you will really have to cosset it, since colds will at once settle in that area.

Very often, Taureans have a fairly slow metabolism. To prevent excessive weight gain, make sure that you exercise regularly. It is important to remember, too, that Taurus may have given you a sweet tooth, so control your intake of heavy, rich cakes and chocolates.

## Planning ahead

Your luxury-loving instincts will decree that you need to earn a lot of money. Fortunately, your Moon sign endows you with a very good financial instinct, and you should follow it. You

**The Moon in Taurus**

will probably know intuitively when to invest and what to invest in, and will not overextend yourself in any one area.

A credit balance on your bank statement will give you much satisfaction (and proof of hard work well done); you will also be anxious to make your money work for you.

### Parenthood

You will make a good parent, but will not allow your children to waste time. Both Leo and Taurus are disciplined signs, so you will be fairly strict with your offspring – at times, you may even be a little hard on them. Your children will certainly know where they stand with you: What you say is exactly what you mean. There will be no nonsense. But think carefully about this; sometimes you might just be too inflexible. Try to keep abreast of your children's opinions, and make sure that you try to move with the times. Otherwise, in spite of an excellent set of values, you may encounter great difficulties.

# THE MOON IN
# GEMINI

YOUR LEO CREATIVITY COULD BLEND WITH YOUR GEMINIAN GIFT
FOR COMMUNICATION AND MAKE YOU A WRITER. DO
NOT QUESTION YOUR EMOTIONS OR TALK SO MUCH THAT
THERE IS NO TIME FOR ACTION.

The fire of your Leo Sun is fanned and encouraged by your air sign Geminian Moon, which makes you respond to situations in a powerful, rational, and intellectual way. You are very quick-witted, and always ready with some clever and original remark. The Leo tendencies to formality and pomposity are unlikely to emerge in your personality.

## Self-expression

You are extremely versatile and may tend to flit – perhaps too readily – from one interest or project to the next. Try to avoid superficiality and falling into the trap of leaving a clutter of unfinished tasks and abandoned hobbies in your trail.

Your Leo creativity could find expression through writing or perhaps in some glamorous craftwork – using, for instance, precious or semiprecious stones, crystals, metals, or fabrics. You do not lack enthusiasm, but may have

to make a conscious effort to keep it on the boil, since boredom and that uniquely Geminian fault, restlessness, could overtake you.

## Romance

You may question or rationalize your emotions, especially when you first realize that they are awakened. Make quite sure that you do not suppress your emotions altogether, since your whole personality will suffer if you do.

In love, you can be both lighthearted and passionate. When friendship embraces full, physical love, all the notes of your Leo personality will be sounded.

## Your well-being

The Geminian body area covers the hands and arms, which may be particularly vulnerable to accidents; the Geminian organ is the lungs. It is absolutely vital that anyone with a Gemini emphasis who is a smoker

**The Moon in Gemini**

should try to limit or stop the habit. Consult your doctor right away if a cough settles on your lungs.

### Planning ahead

Leos love quality goods, and need to earn as much money as possible. You may be attracted to moneymaking schemes with speedy and generous returns on capital. Be cautious: You could lose more than you gain. Take professional advice in these matters. Because you are among the most versatile of Leos, you may want to organize your life to ensure that you have two different sources of income. You could, for instance, take a hobby to professional standards and then go on to market it in some way.

### Parenthood

You will probably be among the liveliest of Leo parents, since Gemini has the reputation of being the most youthful sign of the Zodiac. You will be young at heart (and probably body), and your children will appreciate the fact.

# THE MOON IN
# CANCER

THE SUN AND MOON ARE IN THE SIGNS THAT THEY RULE, AND
YOU THEREFORE HAVE A PERFECT BLEND OF POSITIVE AND
NEGATIVE ELEMENTS. USE YOUR LEO SELF-EXPRESSION, AND
FOLLOW YOUR CANCERIAN INTUITION AND INSTINCTS.

The Sun and Moon, the two most powerful bodies in the Solar System, work very strongly and well for you; their influences combine to give you some excellent personality traits that you should always aim to use to your full advantage.

## Self-expression

Your Cancerian Moon adds a very potent intuition to your Leo Sun sign characteristics and powerful instincts that you should nurture. If you instinctively feel that you should take a certain line of action, then go ahead and do so. Your Moon sign also gives you a very powerful and vivid imagination that should be expressed creatively in some way.

By harnessing this quality, you may well produce some great work in arts and crafts. But take care that you do not let your imagination get out of hand, since you have a tendency to worry unnecessarily.

## Romance

Your emotions are highly charged: The fiery, assertive, and enthusiastic emotion of Leo is joined by the more tender, sensitive emotion of the Moon in Cancer. You will not find it difficult to express your feelings to your loved ones, be they lovers, children, or a household pet. Your protective instinct is also very strong, and while you are a wonderfully exuberant and passionate lover, you may at times tend to smother your partners. Be careful, because you may create a claustrophobic atmosphere within your relationships.

## Your well-being

You are far more prone to worry than most Leos. To counter any unnecessary anxiety, allow your Leo optimism plenty of free expression.

The Cancerian body area covers the chest and breasts. Women with this emphasis should examine their

**The Moon in Cancer**

breasts regularly – although it is important to realize that it is mere coincidence that the name of the sign is the same as that of the disease.

## Planning ahead

Your Cancerian Moon gives you an instinctive business sense. You are able to invest wisely and shrewdly, although you could feel a certain amount of conflict in this area. The Leo you is very generous and enjoys spending money on pleasure and beautiful things, while your Cancerian instinct tends to make you more careful with money. A fascinating and very lucrative hobby for you could be to start an unusual collection of some kind, of objects that will increase in value over the years. This will make positive use of your Cancerian hoarding instinct.

## Parenthood

You will be a very sensible and enthusiastic parent, and will encourage your children to express their own potential as fully as possible. Try not to be overprotective toward them, and allow them to leave the nest and make their own lives when they feel the need.

# THE MOON IN
# LEO

BECAUSE BOTH THE SUN AND THE MOON WERE IN LEO ON THE
DAY OF YOUR BIRTH, YOU WERE BORN UNDER A NEW
MOON. LEO IS A FIRE SIGN, AND THIS ELEMENT POWERFULLY
INFLUENCES YOUR PERSONALITY AND REACTIONS.

Should you study a list of your enthusiastic, optimistic, and positive Sun sign, you will realize that a great many apply to you. On average, out of a list of, say, 20 Sun sign characteristics, most people will identify with 11 or 12. For you the average increases considerably, because the Sun and Moon were both in Leo when you were born.

### Self-expression

Your Sun sign makes you very positive in outlook and gives you exceptional organizing ability, plus a great deal of creative potential. Your Moon influence adds a powerful instinctive urge to express these qualities fully. Bear in mind also that since there is an additional emphasis on the fixed quality of Leo, you may sometimes be inflexible.

You will react to most situations in a very Leo way, expressing the ability to take over at a moment's notice –

especially in a crisis. You can also be extremely bossy and dogmatic. Pay attention if you are accused of these unattractive characteristics.

### Romance

You have a great deal of positive, fiery emotion that you express with great intensity in your relationships. Your zest for love and sex is great, but you will see to it that both you and your partner also enjoy a lifestyle highlighted by as many enjoyable events as you can (or possibly cannot) afford. Be careful not to dominate your relationships too powerfully.

### Your well-being

Everything that has been said about Leo health on pages 22 to 23 really does apply to you. Make sure that you take enough exercise to keep your system, and especially your spine and heart, in good working order.
Your liking for rich living could cause

**The Moon in Leo**

weight gain, so keep moving. This will also help to ensure that your circulation remains good. You no doubt love sunshine and warm weather, and hate the cold. While you will probably tan well, remember to protect your skin with a powerful sunscreen cream or makeup.

**Planning ahead**

Because you like to do things in a refreshingly extravagant way, you will spend a lot of money, and so you need to earn plenty of it. Let your financial motto be "great oaks from little acorns grow," and get pleasure from small

investments. Financial security is important to you, and although you tend to be extravagant you probably do not lack business sense.

**Parenthood**

Leo is the sign of parenthood and children, and you will make an excellent parent provided that you avoid being too dogmatic in your attitude. Your interest, encouragement, and enthusiasm will help build a really good relationship between you. You should try to keep abreast of your children's ideas, and you will minimize the generation gap.

# THE MOON IN
# VIRGO

A CAUTIOUS, SOMEWHAT DAMNING INNER VOICE MAY CRITICIZE
YOUR ACTIONS AND SAP YOUR SELF-CONFIDENCE. YOUR
INNER LEO SUN MUST COMBAT THIS INFLUENCE TO ALLOW YOUR
VIRGOAN MOON TO BE CONSTRUCTIVE AND HELPFUL.

Your earth sign Moon, while not particularly in harmony with your fire sign Sun, gives you a marvelously practical instinct that can stabilize the exuberance of your Leo Sun.

## Self-expression
Your natural caution acts as a brake when you are tempted to show off or behave raucously. However, when confronted with a challenge, you sometimes feel a certain apprehension or lack of self-confidence. This is uncharacteristic for most Sun sign Leos, but it could happen in your case due to the influence of your Moon sign. If such a situation occurs, think of your achievements and allow yourself some pride.

You are very logical, with a powerful critical streak, and can cope better with detail than most Sun sign Leos. You will, however, have a tendency to be swamped by the minutiae of a project. Your Leo creativity may well find expression through gardening or craftwork involving natural materials.

## Romance
Your Virgoan Moon will cool your Leo emotions and add a refreshing modesty to your personality.

Despite a passionate Leo nature, caution will be your key word in a developing relationship. Anyone who is attracted to you will be critically dissected before you make a date, and certainly before they are allowed to deepen the relationship.

## Your well-being
Virgo is a sign prone to worry, and more than many Sun sign Leos, you may suffer from this. Your approach should be an analytical one; always assess your problems logically.

The Virgoan body area covers the stomach, and you may have a digestive problem that tends to recur

**The Moon in Virgo**

when you are under stress. You will
have a great deal of nervous energy,
and should this result in tension, you
may be prone to migraines. If this is
the case, a relaxation technique such
as yoga could be of help.

**Planning ahead**
Your Virgoan Moon will be a vital
influence when it comes to finance.
Leo extravagance is less likely to
affect you than other Sun sign Leos.
Sometimes you will be better off than

you realize; while you should not
waste money, do not deny yourself
things that make life enjoyable.

**Parenthood**
While all Sun sign Leos have fun with
their children, be careful that you are
not too critical of their efforts. Such
criticism can lead to ebbing self-
confidence in a youngster. If you
respond to the younger generation's
opinions and attitudes, you will not
suffer from generation gap problems.

# THE MOON IN
# LIBRA

WITH YOUR MOON IN LIBRA, YOU MAY SEEM LAZY OR DISTANT
TO CASUAL OBSERVERS, BUT A LEO SUN NEEDS
TO LIVE EVERY DAY TO THE FULL. YOUR MOON WILL
ALSO HELP YOU TO ENJOY LIFE.

The combination of the fire element of your Sun and the air element of your Moon add some fascinating aspects to your personality.

### Self-expression

You will respond to challenges with typical Leo enthusiasm. Your Libran Moon will ensure that this enthusiasm will be governed and controlled in a calm, relaxed, and diplomatic way.

With indecisiveness being the worst Libran fault, you may have uncharacteristic second thoughts, especially under pressure or in a stressful situation. At such times, use your Leo organizing ability. It will enable you to take control of your thinking processes.

Both Leos and Librans love the good life, comfort, and luxury. In this area you will experience no conflict between your Sun and Moon signs; you have the ability to sit back, relax, and simply enjoy being sociable.

### Romance

You make a wonderful lover, and are, no doubt, very considerate of your partner's needs. In some respects you may not feel psychologically whole until you are settled in a permanent relationship. Be careful: in your desire to relate in depth, you may have a tendency to commit yourself prematurely. At times you could expect too much from your partner, simply because you, yourself, have so much to give.

### Your well-being

The Libran body area covers the kidneys and the lumbar region of the back. Because Leo rules the spine and back, you may well be subject to pain in that area. The quality of the mattress you sleep on is important. You may also tend to get a lot of headaches, which could be due to slight kidney upset. Seek medical advice whenever necessary.

**The Moon in Libra**

Good food is another luxury enjoyed by both Leo and Libra; Librans tend to put on weight more easily, since many have a fairly slow metabolism. If you tend to move in a languid way and walk slowly, make an effort to speed up your metabolism through frequent exercise.

**Planning ahead**

Leo extravagance and love of quality will certainly eat into your finances. Since you may be bored by bookkeeping and investing, you would be wise to seek sound financial advice from an expert and to embark on a sensible saving plan.

**Parenthood**

Do not allow Libran indecisiveness to undermine your positive Leo qualities in your role as a parent. Your Leo Sun sign will ensure that you enjoy parenthood, and your enthusiasm for your children's interests will spur them on to greater effort. Be aware of their concerns and opinions in order to avoid the generation gap.

# THE MOON IN
# SCORPIO

LEO QUALITIES GAIN DEPTH, INTENSITY, AND A POWERFUL,
EMOTIONALLY ORIENTED DRIVING FORCE BY A SCORPIO
MOON. YOU MUST BE TRULY INVOLVED IN YOUR WORK
AND ENJOY A FULFILLING RELATIONSHIP.

Y ou are likely to have very strong resources of both physical and emotional energy and, for the sake of your inner fulfillment, it is vital that your life is rewarding enough to allow them full rein.

## Self-expression
You must be mentally involved in your work. If this is not the case, you will probably feel discontented and growing dissatisfaction will get the better of you.

Both Leo and Scorpio are of the fixed quality, so you may well have to consciously develop the art of being flexible. Try to keep an open mind, and take heed if someone accuses you of being dogmatic or stubborn. Be firm, but not intractable.

## Romance
Possessing both the fiery emotion of Leo and the deep, intense emotion of Scorpio, you will express your feelings very fervently. You will be among the most passionate of lovers and will have a great need for a responsible partner who is as highly sexed as you are. The worst Scorpio fault is jealousy, which is not something that is usually felt by Sun sign Leos. Should you fall prey to it, try to be rational and to allow Leo magnanimity full expression.

## Your well-being
The Scorpio body area is traditionally said to cover the genitals. Regular gynecological examinations are advisable for women and men should examine their testicles regularly, as good preventive measures.

While some people with a Scorpio emphasis are lean and wiry, others tend to be stocky. If you fall into the latter category you may have a slightly slow metabolism. Try to speed it up through exercise. Both Leo and Scorpio like to live life to the full, and

**The Moon in Scorpio**

enjoy quality food and wines. These can, of course, adversely affect your body shape. If you need to lose weight, gradually adjust your general food intake and develop a more sensibly balanced diet.

### Planning ahead
You have excellent business instincts. When investing, you will probably do well by following them. Your Leo and Scorpio fondness for quality and beautiful things is likely to cost you a great deal of money. Therefore a lot of your energy should be geared to making as much money as possible.

### Parenthood
You may be a strict parent. While you will enjoy being with your children, you may be a little too demanding. If you are not dogmatic, you will share a good relationship. As your children grow up, they will develop different opinions to yours, and you should try to accept them.

# THE MOON IN
# SAGITTARIUS

YOUR SUN AND MOON SIGNS OFFER A LIVELY COMBINATION, WITH
THE SAGITTARIAN MOON ADDING A CASUAL STREAK
TO THE LEO SUN. YOU NEED ADVENTURE IN STUDY AND TRAVEL,
AND YOU WILL COPE WITH DAUNTING CHALLENGES.

Provided that you are consciously aware of one or two negative tendencies, you should be able to make your Leo Sun and Sagittarian Moon work together for you.

### Self-expression
You have great positive spirit that surfaces as soon as you are challenged in any way. When someone makes a suggestion that pleases you, you will want to encourage them. As long as you keep your enthusiasm burning bright you will ensure that, together, you will achieve every one of your goals. It is easy for you to grasp the overall picture of any situation immediately, but you should accept the fact that you are rather easily bored by detail.

You are very versatile, and for you to be really happy with this area of your personality you should have a variety of physical, mental, and creative interests. Your emotions are powerful, and it is good for you to involve yourself in a cause about which you feel strongly.

### Romance
It is in the area of love and relationships that your powerful feelings can be most fully expressed. You may fall in love very quickly – perhaps even at first sight – and your love of life, enthusiasm for love and sex, and warm, affectionate nature will soon break down your prospective partner's defenses. Although you are eager for a permanent relationship, you also have a greater need for freedom of expression than most Sun sign Leos.

### Your well-being
The Sagittarian body area covers the hips and thighs, where most women of this sign tend to put on weight. It is advisable for you to have a fairly light diet. The Sagittarian organ is the

**The Moon in Sagittarius**

liver; as a result you may suffer from hangovers rather more than most Leos if you overindulge.

**Planning ahead**

You may be fascinated by financial risk-taking, or even gambling. Your Leo Sun gives you extravagant tastes, so be careful. Do not risk more money than you can afford to lose, and do not be tempted by get-rich-quick schemes. You could, all too easily and all too quickly, lose a great deal of money. Always be prepared to seek sound professional advice in this area of your life.

**Parenthood**

Although most Leos enjoy parenthood, some tend to be rather formal in their relationships with their children. This is less likely in your case, and you will not find it difficult to enjoy their enthusiasms.

Similarly, while you will not want your children to be clones of yourself, they should not, on the whole, be bored by your own varied interests; Try to develop any creative talent that they inherit. You will be able to keep abreast of their opinions, and should suffer very few problems with the generation gap.

# THE MOON IN
# CAPRICORN

YOU WILL BE AMBITIOUS AND WILL SUCCEED IN WHATEVER YOU
PUT YOUR MIND TO. ALLOW YOUR EARTH SIGN MOON TO
TELL YOU INSTINCTIVELY WHEN TO MAKE IMPORTANT MOVES,
BUT DO NOT LET IT COOL YOUR WARM LEO SUN.

Your Capricornian Moon endows you with qualities that contrast strongly with those of your Leo Sun, but you should be able to blend them and make them work for you.

### Self-expression
Caution and a serious, well-considered response to most situations are characteristic of you, and your Leo enthusiasm will be controlled by a practical and cool approach to important issues. But your Leo love of life will always shine through, and it is extremely likely that you have an instinctive, dry sense of humor that is more amusing than you think.

Your Capricornian Moon may have a slight dampening effect on the warmth of your Leo Sun, making you feel somewhat gloomy and depressed at times. Clouds may darken your psychological landscape until the influence of your Leo Sun takes over.

Leos are generally very ambitious and like to have their own tiny kingdoms to rule. Capricornians can also be extremely ambitious and are always aspiring to rise to greater things. If all goes well, this combined attitude will help you achieve whatever you set your heart on.

### Romance
Your Capricornian Moon will make you cautious in your attitude and approach to the opposite sex. Once committed, both Leos and Capricornians are usually faithful. But you may not be averse to a little social climbing, and you should curb any tendency to show off.

### Your well-being
The Capricornian body area covers the knees and shins. If you suffer from stiffness of the joints, exercise may help. The teeth are also Capricorn-ruled, so make sure you

**The Moon in Capricorn**

have regular dental checkups. Your skin may tan less easily than that of most Leos, so wear a good sunscreen.

**Planning ahead**
While your Leo Sun urges you to spend and enjoy your money, your Capricornian instincts will encourage you to take a practical line and make you a wise investor. You probably have good business sense, and could do well if you start your own business. For you the most important thing is to enjoy your money. Do not waste time

and energy spending it simply to impress other people. Spend it, instead, on your loved ones. Your Moon will work for you and prevent you from spending unwisely.

**Parenthood**
If your children ever accuse you of being pompous or a fuddy-duddy, be sure to take note. Avoid being so involved with making money for them and trying to provide everything they need, that you miss out on really knowing them.

# THE MOON IN
# AQUARIUS

LEO AND AQUARIUS ARE POLAR OR OPPOSITE ZODIAC SIGNS, SO YOU
WERE BORN UNDER A FULL MOON. YOU COULD SUFFER FROM
PERIODS OF RESTLESSNESS, AND YOU MUST AVOID BEING STUBBORN.
LET AQUARIAN ORIGINALITY IGNITE LEONINE CREATIVITY.

Each of us, in some way, expresses elements of our polar or opposite sign, the sign that lies across the Zodiac from our Sun sign.

For Leo, the polar sign is Aquarius, and because the Moon was in that sign when you were born, the polarity is emphasized in a most striking way.

### Self-expression
You have a very independent streak and like to do things in a way that is just right for you. It may be that you have evolved a unique lifestyle that you guard jealously.

You will express your originality in a variety of ways. Perhaps you like to look a little different, or maybe your job is an unusual one. Your Leo creativity could be spiced with originality, and that will make inner fulfillment even more likely for you.

It is important that you develop flexibility; since both Leo and Aquarius are of the fixed quality, that

tends to make you stubborn. Always aim to complete projects, or you will feel dissatisfied and restless. This is one effect of being born at the time of the Full Moon.

### Romance
You may tend to distance yourself from prospective partners, feeling that you are not yet ready for total commitment. However, anyone with an Aquarian influence is also very romantic, and once a partner has paved the way for you, you are capable of very faithful love and a rewarding sex life – if you are given enough room to breathe, and allowed some independence.

### Your well-being
The Aquarian body area covers the ankles, and you may easily twist yours. The circulation is also Aquarius-ruled, and since this is so strongly related to the heart, the Leo

**The Moon in Aquarius**

organ, you should make sure that your blood flows freely. You probably like cold, crisp weather more than most Leos, and may enjoy winter sports.

### Planning ahead
You could be attracted to very glitzy things, such as unusual mirrors, vases, executive toys, high-fashion clothes, and jewelry. These can prove expensive and not very durable and, as a result, your finances may suffer. Try to develop a practical attitude toward money, and seek professional financial advice when you have any cash to invest.

### Parenthood
You will be a lively parent, but your unpredictability may leave your children uncertain where they stand with you. You may want to test new theories by bringing them up in an unusual way. This may work well, but some children feel more secure with a strict set of rules to live by.

# THE MOON IN
# PISCES

YOUR HIGHLY EMOTIONAL LEO FIRE SIGN IS SENSITIZED BY THE
EMOTION OF YOUR WATER SIGN PISCEAN MOON. IF YOU ARE
DISCIPLINED AND CHANNEL YOUR SUPERB RESOURCES, YOU WILL
ACHIEVE A GREAT DEAL IN CREATIVE OR CARING WORK.

While your Sun and Moon signs suggest very different qualities, there is also great sympathy between them, which is emphasized by emotion and creative potential.

### Self-expression
At times you could feel pretty unsure of yourself. It is very important for you to realize that you could deceive yourself. Do not doubt yourself, or resort to putting yourself down. Allow your Piscean Moon to be a source of inspiration and imagination; channel its force creatively. However you do this, express your abundant potential with all the Leo confidence in the world. Be bold, and you will achieve inner fulfillment.

### Romance
You have a very powerful emotional energy that you may, to an extent, express toward humanitarian causes and in the relief of suffering, but it will mostly be directed toward your partner. You are capable of a really grand passion, reaching heights of happiness and the depths of despair.

There is a great dramatic sense in your attitude toward your lover – this is present in most Sun sign Leos, and in your case is made even more colorful by your Piscean Moon. You will be very sensitive to your partner's needs. Learn to be open about your own needs, since you know the things that give you pleasure, and you should not hold back.

### Your well-being
The Piscean body area covers the feet. Do not hesitate to spend money on visits to the podiatrist if you have problems with your feet.

It can be difficult for those with a Piscean influence to be disciplined. When it comes to exercise and regular meals you may, for instance, simply not bother if you are alone. Try to get

**The Moon in Pisces**

into and stick to a regular routine; the Leo in you really needs it, if you are to express your potential fully. Any exercise that inspires you will do you good in both body and soul, and by exercising you will overcome a Piscean vulnerability to flabbiness.

### Planning ahead

Being both very generous and something of a soft touch, you are probably less talented with money than many Leos. Remember, however, that some people will take advantage of you, so be firm if they ask for a loan. While you should seek financial advice before investing, you may wish to put money into building a specific collection of some kind. This will be fun and, if properly managed, it could be a good investment in itself.

### Parenthood

You will be a sympathetic, enthusiastic, and encouraging parent, but do not allow your sensitive reactions to your children's needs and suggestions to get the better of you. Keep in tune with their ideas and concerns, and you will be able to bridge the generation gap.

# MOON CHARTS

THE FOLLOWING TABLES WILL ENABLE YOU TO DISCOVER YOUR
MOON SIGN. THEN, BY REFERRING TO THE PRECEDING
PAGES, YOU WILL BE ABLE TO INVESTIGATE ITS QUALITIES, AND
SEE HOW THEY WORK WITH YOUR SUN SIGN.

By referring to the charts on pages 57, 58 and 59 locate the Zodiacal glyph for the month of the year in which you were born. Using the Moon table on this page, find the number opposite the day you were born that month. Then, starting from the glyph you found first, count off that number using the list of Zodiacal glyphs (below, right). You may have to count to Pisces and continue with Aries. For example, if you were born on May 21, 1991, first you need to find the Moon sign on the chart on page 59. Look down the chart to May; the glyph is Sagittarius (♐). Then consult the Moon table for the 21st. It tells you to add nine glyphs. Starting from Sagittarius, count down nine, and you find your Moon sign is Virgo (♍).

## MOON TABLE

### DAYS OF THE MONTH AND NUMBER OF SIGNS THAT SHOULD BE ADDED

| DAY | ADD | DAY | ADD | DAY | ADD | DAY | ADD |
|-----|-----|-----|-----|-----|-----|-----|-----|
| 1 | 0 | 9 | 4 | 17 | 7 | 25 | 11 |
| 2 | 1 | 10 | 4 | 18 | 8 | 26 | 11 |
| 3 | 1 | 11 | 5 | 19 | 8 | 27 | 12 |
| 4 | 1 | 12 | 5 | 20 | 9 | 28 | 12 |
| 5 | 2 | 13 | 5 | 21 | 9 | 29 | 1 |
| 6 | 2 | 14 | 6 | 22 | 10 | 30 | 1 |
| 7 | 3 | 15 | 6 | 23 | 10 | 31 | 2 |
| 8 | 3 | 16 | 7 | 24 | 10 | | |

## ZODIACAL GLYPHS

| | |
|---|---|
| ♈ | Aries |
| ♉ | Taurus |
| ♊ | Gemini |
| ♋ | Cancer |
| ♌ | Leo |
| ♍ | Virgo |
| ♎ | Libra |
| ♏ | Scorpio |
| ♐ | Sagittarius |
| ♑ | Capricorn |
| ♒ | Aquarius |
| ♓ | Pisces |

| | 1923 | 1924 | 1925 | 1926 | 1927 | 1928 | 1929 | 1930 | 1931 | 1932 | 1933 | 1934 | 1935 |
|---|---|---|---|---|---|---|---|---|---|---|---|---|---|
| JAN | ♊ | ♏ | ♈ | ♌ | ♐ | ♈ | ♍ | ♑ | ♉ | ♎ | ♓ | ♋ | ♏ |
| FEB | ♌ | ♐ | ♉ | ♍ | ♑ | ♊ | ♏ | ♓ | ♋ | ♐ | ♈ | ♌ | ♑ |
| MAR | ♌ | ♑ | ♉ | ♍ | ♒ | ♋ | ♏ | ♓ | ♋ | ♐ | ♉ | ♍ | ♑ |
| APR | ♎ | ♓ | ♋ | ♏ | ♈ | ♍ | ♑ | ♉ | ♍ | ♒ | ♊ | ♎ | ♓ |
| MAY | ♏ | ♈ | ♌ | ♐ | ♉ | ♎ | ♒ | ♊ | ♎ | ♓ | ♋ | ♐ | ♈ |
| JUN | ♑ | ♉ | ♍ | ♒ | ♋ | ♏ | ♓ | ♌ | ♐ | ♉ | ♍ | ♑ | ♊ |
| JUL | ♒ | ♋ | ♏ | ♓ | ♌ | ♐ | ♈ | ♍ | ♑ | ♊ | ♎ | ♓ | ♋ |
| AUG | ♈ | ♌ | ♐ | ♉ | ♍ | ♒ | ♊ | ♏ | ♓ | ♋ | ♐ | ♈ | ♌ |
| SEP | ♉ | ♎ | ♒ | ♋ | ♏ | ♓ | ♌ | ♐ | ♈ | ♍ | ♑ | ♊ | ♎ |
| OCT | ♊ | ♏ | ♓ | ♌ | ♐ | ♉ | ♍ | ♑ | ♉ | ♎ | ♓ | ♋ | ♏ |
| NOV | ♌ | ♑ | ♉ | ♍ | ♑ | ♊ | ♏ | ♓ | ♋ | ♐ | ♈ | ♌ | ♑ |
| DEC | ♍ | ♒ | ♊ | ♎ | ♓ | ♌ | ♐ | ♈ | ♌ | ♑ | ♉ | ♍ | ♒ |

| | 1936 | 1937 | 1938 | 1939 | 1940 | 1941 | 1942 | 1943 | 1944 | 1945 | 1946 | 1947 | 1948 |
|---|---|---|---|---|---|---|---|---|---|---|---|---|---|
| JAN | ♈ | ♌ | ♑ | ♉ | ♍ | ♒ | ♊ | ♎ | ♓ | ♌ | ♐ | ♈ | ♍ |
| FEB | ♉ | ♎ | ♒ | ♊ | ♏ | ♈ | ♌ | ♐ | ♉ | ♍ | ♑ | ♊ | ♎ |
| MAR | ♊ | ♎ | ♒ | ♋ | ♐ | ♈ | ♌ | ♐ | ♉ | ♎ | ♒ | ♊ | ♏ |
| APR | ♌ | ♐ | ♈ | ♌ | ♑ | ♉ | ♎ | ♒ | ♋ | ♏ | ♓ | ♌ | ♑ |
| MAY | ♍ | ♑ | ♉ | ♎ | ♒ | ♊ | ♏ | ♓ | ♌ | ♐ | ♉ | ♍ | ♒ |
| JUN | ♎ | ♒ | ♋ | ♏ | ♈ | ♌ | ♑ | ♉ | ♎ | ♒ | ♊ | ♏ | ♓ |
| JUL | ♏ | ♓ | ♌ | ♑ | ♉ | ♍ | ♒ | ♊ | ♏ | ♓ | ♌ | ♐ | ♈ |
| AUG | ♑ | ♉ | ♎ | ♒ | ♋ | ♏ | ♈ | ♌ | ♐ | ♉ | ♍ | ♑ | ♊ |
| SEP | ♓ | ♋ | ♏ | ♈ | ♌ | ♑ | ♉ | ♍ | ♒ | ♋ | ♏ | ♓ | ♌ |
| OCT | ♈ | ♌ | ♑ | ♉ | ♎ | ♒ | ♊ | ♎ | ♓ | ♌ | ♐ | ♈ | ♍ |
| NOV | ♊ | ♎ | ♒ | ♊ | ♏ | ♈ | ♌ | ♐ | ♉ | ♍ | ♑ | ♊ | ♏ |
| DEC | ♋ | ♏ | ♓ | ♌ | ♐ | ♉ | ♍ | ♑ | ♊ | ♎ | ♒ | ♋ | ♐ |

|        | 1949 | 1950 | 1951 | 1952 | 1953 | 1954 | 1955 | 1956 | 1957 | 1958 | 1959 | 1960 | 1961 |
|--------|------|------|------|------|------|------|------|------|------|------|------|------|------|
| JAN | ♑ | ♊ | ♎ | ♓ | ♋ | ♏ | ♈ | ♌ | ♑ | ♉ | ♍ | ♒ | ♋ |
| FEB | ♓ | ♋ | ♐ | ♈ | ♍ | ♑ | ♉ | ♎ | ♒ | ♊ | ♏ | ♈ | ♌ |
| MAR | ♓ | ♋ | ♐ | ♉ | ♍ | ♑ | ♊ | ♏ | ♓ | ♋ | ♏ | ♈ | ♌ |
| APR | ♉ | ♍ | ♒ | ♊ | ♎ | ♓ | ♋ | ♐ | ♈ | ♌ | ♑ | ♊ | ♎ |
| MAY | ♊ | ♎ | ♓ | ♋ | ♐ | ♈ | ♍ | ♑ | ♉ | ♎ | ♒ | ♋ | ♏ |
| JUN | ♌ | ♐ | ♈ | ♍ | ♑ | ♊ | ♎ | ♓ | ♋ | ♐ | ♈ | ♌ | ♑ |
| JUL | ♍ | ♑ | ♊ | ♎ | ♓ | ♋ | ♏ | ♈ | ♌ | ♑ | ♉ | ♍ | ♒ |
| AUG | ♏ | ♓ | ♋ | ♐ | ♈ | ♍ | ♑ | ♉ | ♎ | ♒ | ♊ | ♏ | ♈ |
| SEP | ♐ | ♈ | ♍ | ♑ | ♊ | ♎ | ♒ | ♋ | ♐ | ♈ | ♌ | ♑ | ♊ |
| OCT | ♑ | ♊ | ♎ | ♓ | ♋ | ♏ | ♓ | ♌ | ♑ | ♉ | ♍ | ♒ | ♋ |
| NOV | ♓ | ♋ | ♏ | ♈ | ♍ | ♑ | ♉ | ♎ | ♒ | ♊ | ♏ | ♈ | ♌ |
| DEC | ♈ | ♌ | ♑ | ♊ | ♎ | ♒ | ♊ | ♏ | ♓ | ♌ | ♐ | ♉ | ♍ |

|        | 1962 | 1963 | 1964 | 1965 | 1966 | 1967 | 1968 | 1969 | 1970 | 1971 | 1972 | 1973 | 1974 |
|--------|------|------|------|------|------|------|------|------|------|------|------|------|------|
| JAN | ♏ | ♓ | ♌ | ♐ | ♈ | ♍ | ♑ | ♊ | ♎ | ♒ | ♋ | ♐ | ♈ |
| FEB | ♐ | ♉ | ♍ | ♒ | ♊ | ♏ | ♓ | ♋ | ♏ | ♈ | ♍ | ♑ | ♉ |
| MAR | ♐ | ♉ | ♎ | ♒ | ♊ | ♏ | ♈ | ♌ | ♐ | ♉ | ♍ | ♑ | ♊ |
| APR | ♒ | ♋ | ♏ | ♈ | ♌ | ♑ | ♉ | ♍ | ♒ | ♊ | ♏ | ♓ | ♋ |
| MAY | ♓ | ♌ | ♐ | ♉ | ♍ | ♒ | ♊ | ♎ | ♓ | ♋ | ♐ | ♈ | ♍ |
| JUN | ♉ | ♎ | ♒ | ♊ | ♏ | ♓ | ♌ | ♐ | ♉ | ♍ | ♑ | ♊ | ♎ |
| JUL | ♊ | ♏ | ♓ | ♌ | ♐ | ♈ | ♍ | ♑ | ♊ | ♎ | ♓ | ♋ | ♐ |
| AUG | ♌ | ♐ | ♉ | ♎ | ♒ | ♊ | ♏ | ♓ | ♋ | ♏ | ♈ | ♍ | ♑ |
| SEP | ♍ | ♒ | ♋ | ♏ | ♓ | ♋ | ♐ | ♉ | ♍ | ♑ | ♊ | ♎ | ♓ |
| OCT | ♏ | ♓ | ♌ | ♐ | ♈ | ♍ | ♒ | ♊ | ♎ | ♒ | ♋ | ♐ | ♈ |
| NOV | ♐ | ♉ | ♎ | ♒ | ♊ | ♏ | ♓ | ♋ | ♐ | ♈ | ♍ | ♑ | ♉ |
| DEC | ♑ | ♊ | ♏ | ♓ | ♋ | ♐ | ♈ | ♌ | ♑ | ♉ | ♎ | ♒ | ♊ |

| | 1975 | 1976 | 1977 | 1978 | 1979 | 1980 | 1981 | 1982 | 1983 | 1984 | 1985 | 1986 | 1987 |
|---|---|---|---|---|---|---|---|---|---|---|---|---|---|
| JAN | ♌ | ♑ | ♉ | ♍ | ♒ | ♊ | ♏ | ♓ | ♌ | ♐ | ♉ | ♍ | ♑ |
| FEB | ♎ | ♒ | ♋ | ♏ | ♈ | ♌ | ♐ | ♉ | ♍ | ♒ | ♊ | ♎ | ♓ |
| MAR | ♎ | ♓ | ♋ | ♏ | ♈ | ♍ | ♑ | ♉ | ♎ | ♒ | ♊ | ♏ | ♓ |
| APR | ♐ | ♈ | ♍ | ♑ | ♊ | ♎ | ♒ | ♋ | ♏ | ♈ | ♌ | ♑ | ♉ |
| MAY | ♑ | ♉ | ♎ | ♒ | ♋ | ♏ | ♓ | ♌ | ♐ | ♉ | ♍ | ♒ | ♊ |
| JUN | ♓ | ♋ | ♐ | ♈ | ♌ | ♑ | ♉ | ♎ | ♒ | ♊ | ♏ | ♓ | ♌ |
| JUL | ♈ | ♋ | ♑ | ♉ | ♍ | ♒ | ♋ | ♏ | ♓ | ♐ | ♉ | ♐ | ♍ |
| AUG | ♉ | ♎ | ♓ | ♋ | ♏ | ♈ | ♌ | ♐ | ♈ | ♎ | ♒ | ♊ | ♎ |
| SEP | ♋ | ♐ | ♈ | ♌ | ♐ | ♊ | ♎ | ♒ | ♊ | ♏ | ♓ | ♌ | ♐ |
| OCT | ♌ | ♑ | ♉ | ♍ | ♒ | ♋ | ♏ | ♓ | ♋ | ♐ | ♉ | ♍ | ♑ |
| NOV | ♎ | ♓ | ♋ | ♏ | ♓ | ♌ | ♐ | ♉ | ♍ | ♒ | ♊ | ♎ | ♓ |
| DEC | ♏ | ♈ | ♌ | ♐ | ♉ | ♍ | ♑ | ♊ | ♎ | ♓ | ♋ | ♐ | ♈ |

| | 1988 | 1989 | 1990 | 1991 | 1992 | 1993 | 1994 | 1995 | 1996 | 1997 | 1998 | 1999 | 2000 |
|---|---|---|---|---|---|---|---|---|---|---|---|---|---|
| JAN | ♊ | ♎ | ♒ | ♋ | ♏ | ♈ | ♌ | ♑ | ♉ | ♎ | ♒ | ♊ | ♏ |
| FEB | ♋ | ♐ | ♈ | ♍ | ♑ | ♉ | ♎ | ♒ | ♋ | ♏ | ♈ | ♌ | ♐ |
| MAR | ♌ | ♐ | ♉ | ♍ | ♒ | ♊ | ♎ | ♓ | ♋ | ♏ | ♈ | ♌ | ♑ |
| APR | ♍ | ♒ | ♊ | ♏ | ♓ | ♋ | ♐ | ♈ | ♍ | ♑ | ♊ | ♎ | ♓ |
| MAY | ♏ | ♓ | ♌ | ♐ | ♈ | ♍ | ♑ | ♉ | ♎ | ♒ | ♋ | ♏ | ♈ |
| JUN | ♐ | ♉ | ♍ | ♑ | ♊ | ♎ | ♓ | ♋ | ♐ | ♈ | ♌ | ♑ | ♉ |
| JUL | ♑ | ♊ | ♎ | ♒ | ♋ | ♐ | ♈ | ♌ | ♑ | ♉ | ♎ | ♒ | ♋ |
| AUG | ♓ | ♌ | ♐ | ♈ | ♍ | ♑ | ♉ | ♎ | ♓ | ♋ | ♏ | ♓ | ♌ |
| SEP | ♉ | ♍ | ♑ | ♊ | ♏ | ♓ | ♋ | ♏ | ♈ | ♌ | ♑ | ♉ | ♎ |
| OCT | ♊ | ♎ | ♒ | ♋ | ♐ | ♈ | ♌ | ♑ | ♉ | ♎ | ♒ | ♊ | ♏ |
| NOV | ♌ | ♐ | ♈ | ♍ | ♑ | ♉ | ♎ | ♒ | ♋ | ♏ | ♈ | ♌ | ♑ |
| DEC | ♍ | ♑ | ♉ | ♎ | ♒ | ♋ | ♏ | ♈ | ♌ | ♐ | ♉ | ♍ | ♒ |

# THE
# SOLAR SYSTEM

THE STARS, OTHER THAN THE SUN, PLAY NO PART IN THE SCIENCE
OF ASTROLOGY. ASTROLOGERS USE ONLY THE BODIES IN THE
SOLAR SYSTEM, EXCLUDING THE EARTH, TO CALCULATE HOW OUR
LIVES AND PERSONALITIES CHANGE.

### Pluto
Pluto takes 246 years to travel around the Sun. It affects our unconscious instincts and urges, gives us strength in difficulty, and may emphasize any inherent cruel streak.

### Neptune
Neptune stays in each sign for 14 years. At best it makes us sensitive and imaginative; at worst it encourages deceit and carelessness, making us worry.

### Uranus
The influence of Uranus can make us friendly, kind, eccentric, inventive, and unpredictable.

### Saturn
In ancient times, Saturn was the most distant known planet. Its influence can limit our ambition and make us either overly cautious (but practical), or reliable and self-disciplined.

PLUTO

NEPTUNE

URANUS

SATURN

### Jupiter

Jupiter encourages expansion, optimism, generosity, and breadth of vision. It can, however, also make us wasteful, extravagant, and conceited.

### Mars

Much associated with energy, anger, violence, selfishness, and a strong sex drive, Mars also encourages decisiveness and leadership.

JUPITER

### The Moon

Although it is a satellite of the Earth, the Moon is known in astrology as a planet. It lies about 240,000 miles from the Earth and, astrologically, is second in importance only to the Sun.

MERCURY

THE MOON

VENUS

MARS

EARTH

### The Sun

The Sun, the only star used by astrologers, influences the way we present ourselves to the world – our image or personality; the face we show to other people.

### Venus

The planet of love and partnership, Venus can emphasize all our best personal qualities. It may also encourage us to be lazy, impractical, and too dependent on other people.

### Earth

Every planet contributes to the environment of the Solar System, and a person born on Venus would no doubt be influenced by our own planet in some way.

### Mercury

The planet closest to the Sun affects our intellect. It can make us inquisitive, versatile, argumentative, perceptive, and clever, but perhaps inconsistent, cynical, and sarcastic.